WHY GOD
Why

Unless otherwise noted, all Scripture quotations are taken from the
New King James Version. Copyright © 1982 by Thomas Nelson,
Inc. Used by permission. All rights reserved.

ISBN: 978-1-950791-52-1

Cover and text layout design: Kristi Yoder

Published by:
TGS International
P.O. Box 355
Berlin, Ohio 44610 USA
Phone: 330.893.4828
Fax: 330.893.2305
www.tgsinternational.com

WHY GOD
Why

LESTER BAUMAN

Table of Contents

Introduction

A woman I'll call Maria once contacted me and complained about God. "God promised me a husband and a family years ago, and He still hasn't done it."

She didn't tell me how God had given her that promise. But I told her that God sometimes says no to our requests.

Maria wasn't very pleased with this. "He promised me," she replied stiffly. "If you think He might not honor that, then you are a false teacher."

I never heard from her again, but I have received other similar complaints since then.

It was soon after this that I started to think about writing this book. Here are a few of the questions I'd like to consider:

- Who is God?
- What can we expect from God?
- Does God ever break His promises?
- Is God obligated to give us what we ask from Him?
- Does He ever say no?
- And if so, why?
- And finally, what does God expect of ME?

I'd like to dedicate this book to Maria and anyone else who has struggled with these questions.

Job Learns About God

Do not be rash with your mouth, and let not your heart utter anything hastily before God. For God is in heaven, and you on earth; therefore let your words be few. Ecclesiastes 5:2

Job's Experience[1]

Job was a good man. So good that God called him blameless and upright. But one day Satan went to visit God, and God told him about Job's goodness.

Satan wasn't impressed. He sneered at God's description.

---

[1] Taken from the Old Testament Book of Job

"Oh, sure. It's no wonder he serves you. You've put a hedge around him so I can't get at him. And you've made him rich; he's the richest man in the East. Let me take away his blessings, and then we'll see what he's really like! He'll curse you to your face."

"Okay," God replied. "I'll let you test him. You can do anything you want to his belongings, but you may not touch him personally."

Satan was sure he could knock Job off his pedestal.

It all happened on the same day. First, a servant came running to tell Job that a band of raiders had swooped in and stolen his oxen—all five hundred teams—and killed the plowmen. They also took five hundred donkeys from a neighboring pasture.

But that wasn't all. Before the first man was finished talking, a second man came running up. "Fire fell from heaven!" he exclaimed. "It burned up all your sheep and the shepherds."

Seven thousand sheep, gone in the snap of a finger. But Job had no time to even think about it before a third man rushed up. "Master, the Chaldeans have stolen your camels and killed the herders!"

Three thousand camels—gone. On top of all the other losses. And in the distance, Job saw another man coming. He was running and waving his arms. Job had just lost all his wealth. What else could have gone wrong? He soon found out.

The messenger fell prostrate at his feet, weeping. "Master," he said, "your ten children were feasting in your oldest son's home and a storm came up. The house collapsed, and all your children are dead."

It was too much. How could a man handle such devastation? Job's cry of anguish came from deep inside. He tore off the robe he was wearing. He shaved his head and fell to the ground in utter grief.

His servants didn't know what to say. They too were devastated. But then, to their astonishment, Job began to pray. "Naked I came from my mother's womb, and naked shall I return there. The LORD gave, and the LORD has taken away; Blessed be the name of the LORD."

The servants looked at each other, shocked.

Satan went back to see God.

God looked at him. "Have you noticed my servant Job? He is still blameless and upright, despite your actions against him."

Satan sneered again. "Sure, a man will give everything he has to save his life. But if you'd let me touch his body, you would see what he's really like. He'll curse you to your face!"

God looked at him. "He is in your hand. Do what you want, but don't kill him."

Satan went directly back to earth to find Job. He struck him with the most painful affliction he could think of. He covered him with painful boils—from the crown of his head to the soles of his feet. Everything Job did hurt. He couldn't walk; he couldn't sit; he couldn't lie down. He couldn't even eat because he had boils in his mouth. Finally, in agony, he sat in an ash pile—the softest place he could find—and scraped the boils with a broken piece of pottery.

Satan also thought of another way to increase Job's agony.

Job's wife broke under the pressure. She walked up to Job and lashed out at him. "What good does it do to be such a good person? Curse God and die! How can you keep your faith in Him when He treats you like this?"

Job looked at her a moment before replying. "Your words are foolish," he said. "Why should we accept good things from God but reject hardship when He sends it?"

Satan still wasn't finished. But first he let Job stew for a while.

Job had three close friends—men that he trusted, even though they were younger than he was. When he saw them coming to visit him, his heart must have warmed a little. They sat down beside him and mourned with him. For a whole week, no one said anything. Then Satan lit the fuse on his final bombshell.

Job spoke first. "Why didn't I die when I was born?" The

question came from the depths of his heart, and it seemed like a dam had burst.

"Why wasn't my mother barren? Why wasn't I stillborn or miscarried? Why doesn't God kill me and put me out of my misery?"

As he began to talk, he wept.

Eliphaz, Job's best friend, took a deep breath and started to talk. "Can I tell you the truth? You have taught many others. Can I now teach you?" He paused and looked at Job searchingly. "Why are you in such despair? You have told others that God doesn't destroy the innocent. So now you need to accept what He sends you."

Job had expected sympathy, not this. He immediately caught Eliphaz's meaning.

"I thought surely my friends would be kind to me." Bitterness filled his voice. "I'm innocent and you know it! Admit it, rather than accusing me."

He looked at the sky and addressed God. "Why do you bother with me? Have I sinned?" His voice rose. "Well then, pardon my transgression and let me die!"

Bildad, his next friend, shook his head. "God is fair and just. Your children must have sinned if God destroyed them. God would never have destroyed them otherwise. And if you would repent rather than blame God, He would heal you. God doesn't punish righteous people."

Job shrank visibly, and his reply was muted and cloaked in despair. "I know you are right," he said. "But how can a man be righteous before God? If I'm such a bad person, why doesn't He show me what to do about it?"

He shifted on his bed of ashes, trying vainly to find a more comfortable position. "Surely this ought to be a two-way street. Why doesn't God do His part?"

Zophar, Job's third friend, looked horrified. "You are full of words," he said. "Words won't vindicate you, nor will empty talk." He shook his head at the very thought.

Job clenched his fist, then released it as the pain from the boils shot through his hand. "Oh, you are such wise men, you three," he said bitterly. "When you die, all wisdom will have left the earth."

He ignored the pain for a moment and sat upright, his eyes flashing. "I'm not inferior to you, and you know it. You forge lies. You are worthless physicians. Why don't you just be quiet?"

He slumped again, then continued more quietly. "A man is like a flower. He lives only a short while, then fades away and dies. But that's not the end. Even a tree will sprout again if it is cut down. I will die, but that won't be the end. I will see God face to face."

His three friends weren't ready to accept Job's answers, and the conversation became more and more heated. Angry words flew back and forth as Job tried to understand and make his friends understand. "How long are you going to torment me? Even my wife despises me. Can't you have any pity on me, your old friend?"

It was a cry of anguish, but his friends were relentless.

"Your wickedness is great . . ."

"Your iniquity is without end . . ."

"You have sent widows away empty . . ."

"God sees your sins; you can't hide from Him . . ."

Job would have torn out his hair, but he had shaved his head. "If I could only go back to the old days when younger men hid themselves because of my greatness, instead of accusing me. Back then, men listened to my counsel."

His voice rose. "Now you mock me. Even though you are younger, you think you know more than your elders.

"I tell you, I'm not a wicked person. I won't even look at a woman! I've given to the poor and the widows. I've avenged the downtrodden."

He shrieked his final words at them. "I want God to answer me! Let Him write a book about me if I have done so many bad things!"

A fourth man had joined them during the discussion, another friend who had come to see Job. He had listened, astonished at the heat of the discussion. He looked at Job, who had buried his head in his hands. He looked at Job's three friends, but they had run out of arguments.

So Elihu began to talk . . .

He rebuked Job and his friends for their presumption about God. He waxed eloquent in his defense of God's character. But Job heard very little of what he was saying.

"Behold, God is mighty, but despises no one . . ."

"Stand still and consider the wondrous works of God . . ."

"With God is awesome majesty . . ."

"He is excellent in power; in judgment, and abundant justice . . ."

His voice droned on, and on, and on, increasing in volume as he tried to get through to Job. But Job was beyond understanding him or responding.

Of course God was great. Of course God was good. Of course God was majestic. Of course God was powerful . . . Job knew all that.

If only they would all go away and leave him to die.

But suddenly the wind picked up and the ashes started to fly. The temperature started to chill noticeably. Something unusual was happening and even Job looked up.

A whirlwind, Job thought. *Like the one that destroyed my son's house. What is going to happen now?*

The wind picked up some more and started to whistle. Grass and sand started to fly, and a miniature sandstorm of ashes whirled around them, causing all five of the men to cover their faces.

Then . . .

"Who is this who darkens counsel by words without knowledge?"

The Voice came from within the whirlwind—deep, majestic, demanding attention.

Is He speaking to me? Job's eyes widened, but he had no time to answer before the Voice continued.

"Now prepare yourself like a man; I will question you, and you shall answer Me."

Job shuddered and bowed his head.

"Where were you when I laid the foundations of the earth?"

"Who shut in the sea . . . when it burst forth?"

"Where is the way to the dwelling of light?"

The questions continued to bombard him. Questions that Job had no idea how to answer. He slumped lower and lower, until suddenly . . .

"Shall the one who contends with the Almighty correct Him? He who rebukes God, let him answer it."

Job knew he had gone too far. In the heat of the argument, he had assumed that he understood more than he did.

But the Voice was waiting for his response. He almost whispered. "Behold, I am vile; What shall I answer You? I lay my hand over my mouth. Once I have spoken, but I will not answer; Yes, twice, but I will proceed no further."

The Voice wasn't finished, and an earlier statement was repeated.

"Now prepare yourself like a man; I will question you, and you shall answer Me: Would you indeed annul My judgment? Would you condemn Me that you may be justified?"

The questions went on and on. Job knew that he had no recourse. In comparison to God, he was nothing—a nobody. He was ignorant and helpless.

When the Voice stopped, Job prostrated himself painfully before the whirlwind. "I have uttered what I did not understand; things too wonderful for me, which I did not know. I abhor myself and repent in dust and ashes."[2]

> But indeed, O man, who are you to reply against God?
> (Romans 9:20)

What Did Job Learn About God?

It doesn't appear that Job ever learned why these things happened to him. God never did reply to Job's request for answers. God didn't give him a list of his sins and errors. Instead, Job was given a brief glimpse of who God is— His greatness and majesty. Job was so overwhelmed that

---

[2] Conversation paraphrased from the Book of Job, NKJV.

he forgot all about his demands.

Instead, he realized that God was so great that it was safe to trust Him. He didn't need answers. He just needed God.

Who Is God?

*The eternal God is your refuge, and underneath are
the everlasting arms. Deuteronomy 33:27*

An Informal Definition of God

The Bible has many definitions of God. But we can draw
some simple concepts from the introductory verse above.

According to this verse, God is each of the following:

- **Eternal** – This means God had no beginning and will
  have no end. He simply *is*.

- **God** – We will discuss this concept more later, but

God is the Supreme Being—the Creator. He is the Object of the Christian's faith.

- **A refuge** – God is a place of safety. He is Someone you can go to when things are going wrong.

- **Our security** – This passage pictures God holding us up in His arms.

While the Bible describes God as judging evil and hating sin, He is also definitely a God who wants men and women to be saved and delivered from sin. He is not a vindictive God who promotes hatred. Neither is He a weakling who is easily pushed around.

Our biggest problem in relating to God begins when we start attributing our own imaginary ideas to Him. This is the major concern we are addressing in this book. This leads us to the next question.

What Kind of God Do You Have?

Many people seem to assume that God exists mainly to make life easier or more pleasant for them. When He doesn't do this, they retaliate by snubbing Him, bribing Him, or trying to put Him on a guilt trip. Or they may threaten to lose their faith in Him, hoping to coerce Him into listening to them.

Unfortunately, all this only shows how little they know about God.

Does God Know My Needs?

*Behold, God is mighty, but despises no one; He is
mighty in strength of understanding. Job 36:5*

Years ago, Chick Publications published a tract containing a picture of a man kneeling beside his bed. The heading was something like, "A Modern-Day Saint Battles the Powers of Darkness."

The man's prayer? "Lord, about that lottery ticket I bought. You know we *need* that money . . ."

As this story illustrates, many people calculate their needs in dollars and cents. This is a problem, from several perspectives. First, many of these needs are merely *wants*. God might be more inclined to answer our prayers if we were praying for food for our children's next meal. But when we want God to finance something like a trip, a boat, a car, or a new computer, God looks at it somewhat differently.

The second problem with calculating needs in terms of dollars and cents is this: *Many times, our real needs are spiritual rather than natural.* Instead of needing a new car, we need to learn to be content with what we have. Instead of a trip, we need to learn to enjoy life at home. Instead of new golf clubs, we need to learn to think about the needs of others.

This puts God in a predicament. Should He give us what we *want*, or what He knows we *need*?

An unknown author said it this way . . .

I asked for strength that I might achieve;
I was made weak that I might learn humbly to obey.

I asked for health that I might do greater things;
I was given infirmity that I might do better things.

I asked for riches that I might be happy;
I was given poverty that I might be wise.

I asked for power that I might have the praise of men;
I was given weakness that I might feel the need of God.

I asked for all things that I might enjoy life;
I was given life that I might enjoy all things.

I got nothing that I had asked for,
But everything that I had hoped for.

Almost despite myself, my unspoken prayers were answered;
I am, among all men, most richly blessed.

Often our biggest problem is that we are ignorant of our real needs, and when God tries to show us, we become angry with Him.

When Jesus faced the cross, He went to the Garden of Gethsemane and prayed. He asked God to let Him avoid the cross. His humanity dreaded the pain, the agony, the scoffing, and the ridicule He knew He would experience. Can you blame Him? Have you ever faced anything close to that? Yet Jesus said, "Not my will, but thine be done." He was ready to accept God's evaluation of the situation.

What about us?

Does God Understand Me?

The LORD your God is gracious and merciful, and will not turn His face from you if you return to Him. 2 Chronicles 30:9

Many People Feel Misunderstood

For instance . . .

"My parents don't understand me." Alfreda was talking to her best friend. Tears were running down her cheeks. "They don't trust me," she added. "All the other girls are going camping overnight. But my father thinks I'm too young to go."

"My parents don't understand me." Johnny glowered at his friend. "They won't buy me a mountain bike like Jack's parents bought for him. My father says my bike is still working well, and I don't need a new one."

In the meantime, Alfreda's mother was talking with her husband. "You don't seem to understand what I'm trying to say." Her shoulders slumped. "All the rest of my family will be at the reunion. Surely plane tickets wouldn't cost that much."

Her husband walked to the window and stared out, not seeing a thing. *She doesn't understand. I'd like to take the family on that trip, but we don't have enough money.*

Down the road, in his little office in the back of the church, Pastor Brown was kneeling at his worn office chair. "Father, I just can't take the pressure anymore. No one seems to understand my concerns about the direction the church is going."

When We Feel No One Understands Us

Children feel their parents don't understand, husbands feel their wives don't understand them, and wives feel frustrated because their husbands can't seem to understand them.

Job felt that his friends didn't understand him. But even worse, God no longer seemed to understand. If you can't trust God to be fair and understanding, who can you trust?

That is the dilemma many people are facing. The bottom is falling out of their lives, and God seems to be sitting back twiddling his thumbs. One girl wrote to me saying, "God gave me my dreams, but now He's not helping me fulfill them."

It seemed to me that God had already fulfilled many of her dreams. But she was sure He should be doing more for her.

Does God Understand Us?

Psalm 139

[1] O Lord, You have searched me and known me.

[2] You know my sitting down and my rising up; You understand my thought afar off.

[3] You comprehend my path and my lying down, and are acquainted with all my ways.

[4] For there is not a word on my tongue, but behold, O Lord, You know it altogether.

[5] You have hedged me behind and before, and laid Your hand upon me.

[6] Such knowledge is too wonderful for me; it is high, I cannot attain it.

[7] Where can I go from Your Spirit? Or where can I flee from Your presence?

[8] If I ascend into heaven, You are there; if I make my bed in hell, behold, You are there.

[9] If I take the wings of the morning, and dwell in the uttermost parts of the sea,

[10] Even there Your hand shall lead me, and Your right hand shall hold me.

[11] If I say, "Surely the darkness shall fall on me," even the night shall be light about me;

[12] Indeed, the darkness shall not hide from You, but the night shines as the day; the darkness and the light are both alike to You.

[13] For You formed my inward parts; You covered me in my mother's womb.

[14] I will praise You, for I am fearfully and wonderfully made; marvelous are Your works, and that my soul knows very well.

[15] My frame was not hidden from You, when I was made in secret, and skillfully wrought in the lowest parts of the earth.

[16] Your eyes saw my substance, being yet unformed. And in Your book they all were written, the days fashioned for me, when as yet there were none of them.

[17] How precious also are Your thoughts to me, O God! How great is the sum of them!

[18] If I should count them, they would be more in number than the sand; when I

God made us, so of course He understands us. Look at the following statements, paraphrased from Psalm 139.

- God knows when I sit down and when I get up.

- God knows all my thoughts and actions.

- God sees me when I am traveling and when I stay at home.

- God knows what I am going to say even before I say it.

- God goes ahead of me and follows behind me.

- I can't get away from God's Spirit or His presence.

- Whether I fly into the heavens, or dive to the bottom of the deepest ocean, God is there with me.

- Even in the darkness, I cannot hide from God.

- God made me in my mother's womb, and He will follow me until I die.

God knows *everything* about us. The problem is not that

God doesn't understand us. The problem is that *we* don't understand *Him*. The girl I just mentioned was sure that God had given her the dreams she had because He wanted her to do great things. But maybe she didn't understand Him and what He was saying to her. Perhaps the things she considered great weren't as important to God. Maybe He had great things for her to do that she was considering too small.

Is God Really a Good God?

For the LORD your God is God of gods and Lord of lords,
the great God, mighty and awesome, who shows no
partiality nor takes a bribe. Deuteronomy 10:17

Here are some questions people often use to try to corner God or His followers:

Is God *Good?*

What does it mean to be good? Jesus gave an interesting illustration of God being good. He said . . .

"Ask, and it will be given to you; seek, and you will find; knock, and it will be opened to you. For everyone who asks receives, and he who seeks finds, and to him who knocks it will be opened. Or what man is there among you who, if his son asks for bread, will give him a stone? Or if he asks for a fish, will he give him a serpent? If you then, being evil, know how to give good gifts to your children, how much more will your Father who is in heaven give good things to those who ask Him!" (Matthew 7:7-11).

Let me give you another illustration before we talk about this one. A boy I will call Johnny decided he would like to make some money. He had a good motive—he wanted to help his widowed mother make ends meet. So he asked if she would let him work for a neighboring farmer who went to their church.

Johnny's mother talked to the farmer, and he agreed to hire Johnny. In fact, he could start the following Saturday.

Johnny got up early on Saturday morning. He packed a lunch and off he went. The farmer told him he would like him to plant some pumpkins and walked out to the field with him to show him how he wanted it done.

"I want you to take this stick and poke a hole in the ground," the farmer said. "Then take one pumpkin seed and drop it into the hole. Cover the hole and take two steps down the row toward the end of the field, then do it again. When you get to the end, take several steps sideways, then come up the field doing the same thing again."

Johnny was pleased. This sounded easy. His chest swelled as he thought of the money he would take home to his mother at the end of the day.

The farmer watched him plant several seeds and smiled. "It will be pretty warm by the time you get done," he said. "If you want to, you can take a dip in the creek then." He walked back to the barn, leaving Johnny by himself.

Johnny kept on working. Soon he was at the end of the field and stopped for a little break. He looked at the seeds in his pail and then at the other end of the field. *Wow, this is a big field,* he thought. But he squared his shoulders and started in again.

Punch a hole; drop a seed. Punch a hole; drop a seed. Punch a hole; drop a seed.

For some reason, the second row seemed to take longer than the first. And it was getting warm. He wiped the sweat from his forehead and glanced at the sky. Surely it must be almost lunchtime. But no, the sun wasn't even halfway to the top yet.

He glanced at his pail. "It is going to take a long time to empty this pail," he muttered. But pumpkin seeds don't plant themselves, so he started on his third row. However, his earlier enthusiasm was gone, and this row seemed longer than ever.

He finally reached the other end and looked at his pail again. *I'm going to be here all weekend at this rate,* he thought in despair. The pail looked almost as full as it had when he started. And the field was a lot bigger than he had realized. And the sun? It wasn't even moving in the sky.

He wiped more sweat from his forehead. The sun might not be moving, but it was sure heating him up. He sighed and started half-heartedly on the fourth row of pumpkins.

Punch a hole; drop a seed. Punch a hole; drop a seed. Punch a hole; drop a seed.

About halfway down the row, he noticed that the level in his pail still looked about the same. This was impossible. He was going to die out here in this field. Then he had an idea.

I know what. I'll put two seeds in each hole. That should speed things up.

With renewed enthusiasm he started out again.

Punch a hole; drop two seeds. Punch a hole; drop two seeds. Punch a hole; drop two seeds.

That helped for a while, but not that much. Several rows later he decided this wasn't getting him anywhere, and surely Farmer Joe hadn't realized how long it would take. Maybe he'd never grown pumpkins before. Anyway, it was time to change his routine again.

Punch a hole; drop four seeds. Punch a hole; drop four seeds. Punch a hole; drop four seeds.

That worked for a while, but you guessed it. Soon it was, *punch a hole; drop six seeds. Punch a hole; drop six seeds. Punch a hole; drop six seeds.* Then it became *punch a hole; drop ten seeds. Punch a hole; drop ten seeds.* But counting ten seeds took too long and slowed him down. So he changed the routine again.

Punch a hole; drop a handful . . . Not too big a handful of course, at least not at first. But soon he didn't worry about it anymore. *Punch a hole; drop a handful. Punch a hole; drop a handful.* Now, at last, the pail was emptying at a much more satisfactory rate.

Then he was finished. He noticed uneasily that he had planted only about a third of the field, but he shrugged. Farmer Joe hadn't said he was to plant the whole field, just that he was to plant the pailful of seeds.

Now he could go swimming.

A week went by. For some reason Farmer Joe didn't have as much work for him as he had expected. As Johnny helped his mother in her garden, he enjoyed watching the seeds germinating and the little shoots popping up. That Saturday night, like a flash of light, it suddenly dawned on him that the pumpkin seeds in Farmer Joe's field were also germinating. His face blanched as he thought of the handfuls of seeds he had dropped in those holes. Would they really all grow?

When Johnny went to bed that night, he knelt by his bed and prayed. He asked God to bless his mother and his little sister. He asked God to watch over them that night. Then he gulped a little. "And please, God, would you mind keeping those extra seeds from growing? Please, God!"

Sure enough, the next morning, Johnny almost ran into Farmer Joe at church. He took one look at Farmer Joe's face and knew that God hadn't answered his prayer.

....

This is a simple little story, and you probably chuckled at it. But let's think about it for a little. Doesn't God know what it is like for a young boy to plant a huge field of pumpkins in the hot sun all by himself? Well, maybe the field wasn't huge, but it sure seemed that way to Johnny. And that cool creek had beckoned him all morning. Couldn't God have given him a break? It would have been so easy for Him to stop some of those seeds from growing.

What would you have done if you were in God's shoes? Why? Would a good God really do this for Johnny? Or would He decide that it would be better for Johnny in the long run to learn that the laws of nature are laws, and that what a person sows he will also reap?

Johnny might not have thought of it that way. The point is that what Johnny thought was good for him, and what his mother or Farmer Joe knew was good for him were quite different. It was certainly different from God's perspective. How often do you think God gives us something that He knows will be for our good, even though He knows we won't like it?

So yes, God *is* good if we understand the right definition of the word. People give their children what they need because they love them. God does the same.

I know this doesn't answer all your questions, but stick with me for a little longer.

Is God *God?*

What makes God, God? His power? His greatness? His compassion? Again, we need a definition.

Greta was part of a very poor family. Her mother was a widow, and I think several of her younger sisters were living with them. They all loved God and went to church. But they were so poor that they only had one Bible that they shared together as a family.

Greta loved to read that Bible. She read it every day and often memorized verses from it. She was determined to live for God the best she knew how.

But one day something terrible happened. The chimney started burning, and they couldn't get the fire out. Soon the roof was burning and then the upstairs. Since it was an old house, it went up in flames in a matter of minutes, before the fire department could arrive. Greta and her family lost almost everything they had.

While Greta and her mother and sisters stood there, Greta suddenly realized that their Bible was still in the house. But it was impossible to rescue it now. No one could dash into those flames and come out alive. Greta could think of only one thing to do.

She knelt down right there with all those people around her. "O God!" she prayed. "Please save our Bible! We don't have any money to buy another one."

Wiping away her tears, her mother placed her hand on Greta's shoulder. "God might not save our Bible," she told her daughter, "but He *will* look after us."

But Greta didn't give up. She kept on praying, and when the flames had died down and the embers had cooled, she took a little stick and began digging through the ashes. *We kept our Bible in the living room, right about here,* she told herself. *I'm going to see if I can find it.*

She rooted around some more. Then she felt something under the ashes, and just like that she saw the Bible. It was intact. Completely. Not a scar from the fire. It was a bit warm, but she carefully flipped through the pages. It hadn't been damaged at all.

Greta knelt right there in the ashes and prayed, "Thank you, thank you, thank you, God!"

What do you think? Is God powerful? Powerful enough to be considered GOD. I'm sure Greta thought so. And I'm sure she never forgot that moment.

Is God a *Good God?*

Let's take this proposition a little further. Why did God answer Greta's prayer but not Johnny's? You might have your own ideas, but for some reason Greta's prayer seems more worthy than Johnny's. Maybe that had something to do with it. Johnny needed a lesson in work ethics, and maybe those pumpkin seeds would keep him from getting fired someday. God probably knew he needed that lesson.

God also knew that Greta needed the assurance of His love right at that moment. The greatest comfort He could give her was to save her Bible. I think most people could agree with this analysis.

But things can get more difficult. Life on earth isn't always easy, and many times it seems downright unfair. Let's start with one of the worst ones.

Usually the question starts like this:

If . . .

So right away I know that the writer or speaker has some doubts. But let's carry on.

If God is good . . .

Take a minute to analyze that. The writer is saying, "If this all-powerful, all-knowing Being you call God is kind, benevolent, and caring . . ."

Inevitably the next word is— *Why . . .*

Why, if God is good, does He allow evil?

I know of a young girl who was abducted from her home one night. The perpetrator had one motive: satisfying his selfish, evil lusts. Although she was not killed, this young, innocent girl had a terrifying night as she was sexually molested and scarred for life.

Almost nothing upsets people more than a scenario like this, and these scenarios happen. In fact, they happen regularly. So the question becomes this: *How can God be both God and good at the same time if He allows innocent children to suffer?*

The implication is that God must either be incapable of stopping evil—in which case He isn't God—or unwilling to stop it—in which case He isn't good.

I'm not going to finish answering this question for now, so you have time to think about it. But I will come back to it in the next chapter.

Is God Fair?

*He makes His sun rise on the evil and on
the good, and sends rain on the just and
on the unjust. Matthew 5:45*

Someone once commented to me that his life had gotten worse, rather than better, after he became a Christian. This didn't seem fair to him, especially since some of the people who were mistreating him seemed to be enjoying good success.

Maybe you've felt like that too.

Even some Biblical writers had questions about this. Asaph was a singer and a Levite living at the time of King

David. He wrote twelve different psalms, including the one we are looking at here.

Why Does God Allow Good Things to Happen to Bad People?

Psalm 73 — A Psalm of Asaph

[1]Truly God is good to Israel, to such as are pure in heart.
[2]But as for me, my feet had almost stumbled; my steps had nearly slipped.
[3]For I was envious of the boastful, when I saw the prosperity of the wicked.
[4]For there are no pangs in their death, but their strength is firm.
[5]They are not in trouble as other men, nor are they plagued like other men.
[6]Therefore pride serves as their necklace; violence covers them like a garment.
[7]Their eyes bulge with abundance; they have more than heart could wish.
[8]They scoff and speak wickedly concerning oppression; they speak loftily.
[9]They set their mouth against the heavens, and their tongue walks through the earth.
[10]Therefore his people return here, and waters of a full cup are drained by them.
[11]And they say, "How does God know? And is there knowledge in the Most High?"
[12]Behold, these are the ungodly, who are always at ease; they increase in riches.
[13]Surely I have cleansed my heart in vain, and washed my hands in innocence.
[14]For all day long I have been plagued, and chastened every morning.
[15]If I had said, "I will speak thus," behold, I would have been untrue to the generation of Your children.
[16]When I thought how to understand this, it was too painful for me—
[17]Until I went into the sanctuary of God; then I understood their end.
[18]Surely You set them in slippery places; You cast them down to destruction.
[19]Oh, how they are brought to desolation, as in a moment! they are utterly consumed with terrors.
[20]As a dream when one awakes, so, Lord, when You awake, You shall

despise their image.

21Thus my heart was grieved, and I was vexed in my mind.

22I was so foolish and ignorant; I was like a beast before You.

23Nevertheless I am continually with You; You hold me by my right hand.

24You will guide me with Your counsel, and afterward receive me to glory.

25Whom have I in heaven but You? And there is none upon earth that I desire besides You.

26My flesh and my heart fail; but God is the strength of my heart and my portion forever.

27For indeed, those who are far from You shall perish; You have destroyed all those who desert You for harlotry.

28But it is good for me to draw near to God; I have put my trust in the Lord God, that I may declare all Your works.

In Psalm 73, Asaph confessed that he almost stumbled and that his feet almost slipped. In other words, he almost turned against God.

Why? Let me summarize his struggles . . .

First, he noticed the prosperity of the wicked. Perhaps Asaph was poor, but the wicked people around him were rich. Seemingly they had everything a human heart could desire. They ate so much that their eyes bulged from their fatness!

They weren't in trouble like other people. They scoffed at others. They even spoke loftily about God. "God doesn't know what I'm doing," they said. "He can't stop me!"

And to top it all off, Asaph noticed that *they were always at ease.* There was no sign of guilt.

The more he thought about this, the more confused he became. "All my efforts to live for God are in vain," he wrote. "I have nothing but trouble all day; every new morning just brings me more pain. I could just as well have continued to live in my sins."

Day after day he struggled with his questions, trying to understand what was happening. But it was in vain until he went into God's sanctuary one day. Suddenly he had a flash of insight. He saw that it was the destiny of these people that made all the difference.

He went on to describe the same people again from this new perspective God had given him.

The wicked were on a slippery slope, going downhill. He saw that the road ended at the edge of a cliff, and they were going to plunge over it and be destroyed. Furthermore, he saw that God wasn't impressed at all with their lofty speeches and proud thoughts. He saw right through their shallowness.

Asaph saw how foolish he had been to envy the wicked. Instead, he began to realize how much God had blessed him. God was with him and was guiding him. And someday He would take him home to glory. As he thought on these things, his heart overflowed with praise.

"Whom have I in heaven but You? And there is none upon earth that I desire besides You. . . . It is good for me to draw near to God; I have put my trust in the Lord GOD, that I may declare all Your works" (Psalm 73:25-28).

The next time we are tempted to envy the wicked around

us, let's sit down and count our blessings. If we have Jesus in our heart, what more can we ask for? We have found the greatest prize in existence.

Why Does God Allow Bad Things to Happen to Good People?

Why do innocent children need to suffer? Why do good people get sick? All these bad things and many more happen every day. Is this fair?

Why doesn't God stop evil?

Some people tell you that God doesn't care enough to stop evil. Others tell you that He can't—He doesn't have the power to do it.

Neither of these answers is true. The Bible clearly tells us that God loves us. His heart aches when bad things happen to innocent people. The Bible is also clear that God is all-powerful. It is not a lack of power that keeps God from wiping out evil and evildoers.

So what is it?

Sometime, before time existed, God made a momentous decision. He decided to allow intelligent beings to have the power of choice. Even the angels would have this power. Lucifer, the beautiful and powerful leader of the angels, used this power of choice and turned against God.

A third of the other angels followed him. The first thing they tried to do was overthrow God. The Bible doesn't give us any details about this war with God except to tell us that Lucifer and his angels lost the battle and were driven from heaven.

The chronology of this is a mystery. But somewhere during all of this, God created the universe and man. He decided that humans, too, would have the power to choose to disobey Him. We are not told why, but it seems that God wants all intelligent beings, whether angels or humans, to serve Him voluntarily. He has never forced anyone to serve Him, and He never will.

The ability to choose led to the beginning of evil. Lucifer and his followers were the first to take advantage of it, probably soon after Creation.[1] When he was turned out of heaven, he came to earth determined to take revenge on his loss by persuading Adam and Eve to also choose against God.

He persuaded Eve that having the knowledge of good and evil was worth the risk of offending God. He didn't warn her that the only way to receive the knowledge of evil was through experience. Every human since then has lived under the curse of the knowledge of evil.

This freedom of choice is one reason evil things happen.

Related to this is the fact that *God has put in place natural*

---

[1] I suppose it could have been a little before Creation as well. But it appears that Lucifer fled to earth when he was cast out of heaven.

laws that govern our universe. When we talk about natural laws, we typically think of the laws of nature. But they also include laws like cause and effect, and sowing and reaping. God normally does not interfere with these laws. For instance, an alcoholic can't blame God when he dies from liver disease. Nor should a chronic smoker complain when he contracts lung cancer. Sugar addicts open the door for diabetes, and heavy salt users for strokes.

Similarly, a person who destroys his mind with mind-altering drugs reaps what he has sowed and has no right to blame God for his inability to think straight.

Another natural law that we often do not consider is the law that *evil people will do evil things.* Jesus said in Luke 6:45 that "An evil man out of the evil treasure of his heart brings forth evil. For out of the abundance of the heart his mouth speaks." When an innocent child is tortured to death, or an innocent woman is raped, it is because of the evil in the hearts of people. The governments of this world try to restrain this evil, but they cannot eradicate it. According to 2 Thessalonians 2:6, 7, God restrains evil to a point, but the time will come when He no longer does this.

Unrestrained evil is man's worst nightmare. Even though the world has seen much evil, we still don't know what this would be like.

God *will* judge evil. He *will* eradicate it. But in His own time. Until then, we must live with the choice that Adam and Eve made to allow evil to enter this world.

Is this fair? It doesn't seem that way to us. But God will not coerce people to do His will. He only reserves the right to give them the destiny that they have chosen for themselves. God is holy, and God is just. He is merciful, and He is love. God is good, and He is great. He is fair.[2]

Is It Fair for God to Punish Sinners?

I'm going to lump together several questions that often come up in discussions about God. They are connected but not quite the same.

First: *Is God really giving you a choice when the choice is between submitting to Him or being cast into hell with the devil and his angels?*

Some people feel this is not a realistic choice. They feel neither one is good. They think it is like your mother telling you to either take your cod liver oil or get sick. But did your

---

[2] I have chosen not to use the Romans 8:28 argument that for a Christian everything is either good or produces good. That one is normally used to try to comfort OTHER people, but when bad things strike closer to home, it is a comfortless consolation. I feel better emphasizing the greatness of God rather than the power of positive thinking. There are times when bad things are also the result of mistakes or poor decisions made by good people. Do we really need to find something good in a man driving over his son with a farm tractor in a moment of carelessness? I feel we need to realize that sometimes bad things happen simply because we are humans living in a broken world. We only do damage by trying to justify God by making everything "good."

mother do this because she hated you or wanted to show her authority? No, she did it because she loved you. She didn't want you to get sick.

In the same way, the choice God offers us of serving Him is not a punishment. It is His way of showing us His love. If we stop to think about it, God has done a lot. Can we imagine the excruciating pain Jesus endured on the cross? He did it for you and me—not because He had to, but because He loved us. He did it so our sins could be forgiven and we could live with God in heaven through all eternity, instead of being eternally lost.

Coming to God in genuine repentance and receiving forgiveness of sins through Jesus' sacrifice is the only way to overcome the evil in this world. THIS IS THE ONLY ANSWER TO MAN'S DILEMMA! If we yield to God, we will eventually understand this and be grateful to Him.

It is normal for people to try to find easier and better alternatives to something difficult. As a child, you probably hated cod liver oil. Perhaps you still do. That's why people have developed pills that supply the same nutrients. So now Mom says, "Johnny, take your Omega-3 pills or you will get sick." That's an easier choice, right? Gummy bear vitamins are even better.

Since submitting to God's Word seems so hard, the world has been busy watering it down and packaging it in shiny or sweet capsules. For instance, many churches and theologians now say that sexual sins are permissible as long as no one is hurt. Or war is all right if it is a just war.

But God hasn't produced a second edition of His Word that says that. God's Word still says what it always did. In God's eyes, the choice is still between cod liver oil and getting sick.

But this comparison is not quite accurate. Cod liver oil is truly unpleasant; serving God from the heart is not. Although people imagine that submitting to God must make us miserable, the reality is quite different. Instead of being a burden, it brings rest and peace to our troubled minds. It creates a purpose in life that is impossible to find anywhere else.

Second: *Is it fair for God to condemn people to eternal punishment?*

I think most Christians have wondered about this question. From our human perspective this is hard to swallow or defend. But according to the Bible, God is in control and will do what He decides is best.

There are many things about hell that we don't understand, but the Bible is clear that there is a heaven and a hell, as well as a Day of Judgment that will determine each person's destiny. The Bible also clearly states that God wants everyone to come to Him. At the same time, there is a warning for those who refuse His call.

Romans 9 is a difficult passage—perhaps one of the most difficult passages in the New Testament. In this chapter, Paul uses three illustrations to explain the sovereignty of God over judgment and mercy.

1. In verses 10-14, Paul referred to the account of Jacob and Esau. Before they were born, they struggled with each other in their mother's womb. It became serious enough that their mother, Rebekah, inquired of God about it. He told her she was carrying twins and they would father two nations. These nations would fight each other, but the descendants of the firstborn would serve the descendants of the younger one. Before either of them had done good or evil, God had already decided that Jacob (the younger) would receive mercy, rather than his older brother.

2. In verses 15-18, Paul speaks of God hardening Pharaoh's heart so He could show His power and prove to the people that He is God.

3. Finally, in verses 19-23, Paul uses clay pottery to illustrate how foolish it would be for a pot to tell the potter what it wants to be or how it wants to be used. The potter makes those choices, not the pot.

What is Paul trying to say with these word pictures? Is he really telling us that there is nothing we can do? That God will decide our future and might even make us sinners so He can punish us?

No. Such a picture would not fit with how God is described elsewhere in the Bible. We should note the context of this chapter. Paul was using these illustrations to show the Jews that *God had the right* to bring the Gentiles into His kingdom on an equal basis to the Jews. He also had the right to remove the Jews who were unworthy.

He was not saying that God decides our destiny in advance, and we have no choice in the matter. The Bible clearly states that anyone can come to Christ and be saved.

The third illustration clarifies that God has the right, as God, to call both Jews and Gentiles into His kingdom. He does not decide who to save based on race or bloodline. Instead, Paul insisted that God has the right, *because He is God,* to offer salvation to anyone He chooses, no matter who they are.

We cannot read more into this chapter than it says. It simply tells us that God has reserved the right to make decisions concerning mercy and judgment. We humans sometimes have trouble accepting that we are subject to an overarching authority in these matters, but that is what this chapter tells us.

"But indeed, O man, who are you to reply against God? Will the thing formed say to him who formed it, 'Why have you made me like this?' " (Romans 9:20).

Perspective Is Important

People say faraway pastures look greener. And it often seems that way. When I was a boy, our family was poor. We were one of the homes in our town where local churches went to sing at Christmas time. One year they brought us a big box of groceries, and I remember how I felt when I saw some of my classmates in the group. I don't think it had dawned on me before that we were poorer than our neighbors.

We had an account at the local grocery store, and my mother often sent me with a list to get groceries. I never took any money along, and the storekeeper would ask if I wanted it put on our bill. I never realized until many years later that my mother was embarrassed to go to the store herself because she had no way to pay for what we needed.[3]

A rich family lived at the other end of our town. Their house was a mansion, and their grounds looked like a golf course. In fact, they later sold the property and it was converted into a golf course.

This family had a daughter a little older than I was. From

---

[3] Later, God blessed my parents with the means to pay back the two brothers who owned the store. But for some years those two men quietly fed our family without knowing if they would ever be paid.

my perspective, she seemed to have everything her heart could desire. She didn't flaunt her riches as I recall, but still, she was the rich child in school.

I was quite startled one evening when our school participated in a local concert in a nearby city, and anyone who needed a ride to the destination was to wait in the school basement. As it turned out, the "rich girl" and I were the only ones who didn't have a ride. We sat in the basement of the school together, waiting self-consciously until someone picked us up. Her parents and mine were the only ones who didn't attend the concert.

That should have told me something, but I was too naïve to understand. Several years later, when the rich family went through an explosive marriage breakup, I still didn't understand fully. But looking back, I suspect that the girl I waited with in the school basement would gladly have traded places with me if she could have experienced the happiness I had as a child.

This experience taught me a valuable lesson—things are not always the way they appear. To my immature eyes, the rich girl had it made. She had everything one could want in life. But as I learned later, that was far from true. And because of my lack of understanding, my perspective of her did not reveal the true picture.

That's often the way it is with our understanding of God. Because we don't know His heart and don't understand His great love for us, we end up with a wrong perspective of Him. The only way to see God correctly is to learn to know Him.

Fairness is a matter of perspective.

Can I Trust God?

God is not a man, that He should lie, nor a son of man,
that He should repent. Has He said, and will He not
do? Or has He spoken, and will He not make it good?
Numbers 23:19

Job told his friends, "Though He slay me, yet will I trust Him."

Everything seemed to be going wrong for Job, but he still chose to trust God.

I Can Trust God Because He Loves Me

This is probably one of the best reasons to trust God. When you love people, you will stand by them. You will protect them from evil and help them in any way possible.

But when you really love someone, as a father loves his child, you won't necessarily keep a person from facing difficulties in life. Children don't grow strong without using their muscles.

Nor will you hand your child everything he wants on a silver platter. Not if you really love him. I knew a father who did almost everything for his children. He even paid their car insurance if they ran short of money. The interesting thing was that his children were always running short. They seemingly never had enough money to pay their car insurance.

I'm sure he loved his children. But if he had loved them a little more and encouraged them to face life as it really was, they would probably not have needed his help so much. And they would have felt a lot better about themselves.

I have met people who feel they can't trust God because He hasn't done for them what they wanted. Looking back, I know I didn't always do everything my children wanted me to do for them. I'm sure they sometimes felt that I didn't love them because of decisions I made. But hopefully, as they grew older, they realized it wouldn't have been good for them to always get their own way.

At a time like that, children need to trust their parents. And they will find this much easier if they love their parents and know their parents love them.

It is the same way with God. He has shown His love in many ways. But especially He has shown His love by sending His own Son to die for our sins, so we can be saved. If He loved us enough to do that, we can trust Him in everything else.

We looked at the story of Job in the first chapter. An interesting thought runs through that book. Job was sure that if he could talk to God face to face, he could convince God that he was a good man and that God wasn't being fair to him.

God gave him that chance. He faced up with Job and told him, "Here is your chance. You've said a lot about what you would say to me if you could. Now say it."

You saw Job's response. When he met God face to face, he realized for the first time how great and how good God really was. He had nothing left to say.

I've heard of people listing accusations they would throw in God's face if He ever faced them in judgment. When that time comes, they will realize the same thing Job did. God is so great that they won't have a word to say.

I Can Trust God Because He Is Great

The Bible gives many illustrations of the greatness of God. But since we've been talking about Job, let's go back to him.

In Job chapter 38, after the discussion between Job and his friends hit a stalemate, God arrived on the scene.

God had apparently been evaluating the discussion. In the end, He sided with Job against his friends, but He must have noted that Job had made some strong statements during the discussion. He didn't rebuke Job, but He did ask him some questions.

Many of the questions focused on Job's human limitations. Where was he when God created the world? Oh, and by the way, what are the earth's foundations attached to? And how big is it? Can you make morning come? Have you explored the depths of the sea? Where does light dwell? And what about darkness? Do you know what causes snow? Hail? Do you understand how light is diffused to cause a rainbow? Where does the water come from when it rains?

On and on God went, chapter after chapter. Questions about life, questions about nature, questions about animals, questions about birds, questions about large beasts that we don't know anything about, but which apparently existed in Job's time.

As you read chapters 38-41, you can imagine how Job felt. He had thought he knew a lot. He had been sure he could take on God in a debate to prove his own goodness. He had even insinuated during the discussions with his friends that God wasn't being quite fair. But after he had listened to

God, he knew better.

Job never received an answer to his questions. He may never have found out what this was all about. He didn't need to. He had a glimpse of the greatness of God and that was enough. He could trust God even if he never knew why God had allowed his trials.

God was great. Job wasn't. That was all Job needed to know.

That is all we need to know. Don't take on God. Trust Him instead.

I Can Trust God Because He Is GOD

If you accept that God is God in everything that the word entails, then you will realize that you can trust Him.

In Isaiah 40:9-31, the prophet gives a listing like Job's, but shorter. He contrasts God with an idol and asks his readers what they think God is like. Then he describes an idol made of gold with silver trimmings. Can a man-made lump of gold do what God has done?

A lot of people don't have enough money for an idol made of solid gold, the prophet noted, so these people take a tree that won't rot and get someone to carve it into an image. Whether the idol is solid gold or merely wooden makes little difference. The comparison between the idol and the true God is so obvious that the idol would blush if it could.

The comparison between God and men is similar. The nations are like a drop in a bucket. They are like a bit of dust on a scale. And the people are like grasshoppers before God.

Dust. A drop of water. Grasshoppers. Once we realize how small we are in comparison to God, we are started on the right track to follow Him.

God doesn't snub His nose at men despite this. Instead, He graciously offers us His help. He offers power and strength to the weak. For those who wait on God, He will renew their strength. He will help them fly like eagles. He will help them run and not get tired, and walk without fainting.

Who wouldn't trust a God like this?

Distorted Views of God

God is wise in heart and mighty in strength. Who has hardened himself against Him and prospered? Job 9:4

People often misunderstand God. Some people even believe God was invented by people who worship Him. Because of this, they think God becomes what people want Him to be. After all, He only exists in their minds.

Sometimes this is true. The following sections describe some of the different kinds of gods that people have created for themselves. But remember, if you serve one of these gods, your god really is imaginary—and imaginary gods can't do much for you.

Is God a Magic Genie?

Andrew had a lot of problems in his upper teens. At the university, he got involved in gambling. He evidently wasn't a successful gambler, because he ran up some big gambling debts, and people started to pressure him for the money he owed them. But he didn't have the money to pay them, nor anyone to borrow it from. That was part of the reason he had gambled in the first place.

Apparently Andrew had received a knowledge of God from somewhere, as he did a good thing—he began to pray for help.

But Andrew's knowledge of God fell a bit short at this point. He thought if he prayed long enough and desperately enough, God would supply the money he needed. This didn't happen, and when I talked to him he had almost given up on God.

"God has promised to look after us and provide for our needs," he told me. "Why isn't God giving me the money I need to pay off my debts?"

Andrew's view of God reminds me of an old story.

You may have heard of the *Arabian Nights*, a collection of old tales. The story "Aladdin's Lamp," one of these tales, is about a boy who was drafted by an evil magician to take an old lamp from a cave for him. When Aladdin wouldn't give him the lamp before exiting the cave, the magician trapped him inside and left him to die.

Because he had nothing else to do, Aladdin started to wipe the dust off the lamp. Immediately a genie appeared and told him that he would fulfill any wish that he made. Aladdin used the genie's powers to escape from the cave. He also asked the genie to build him a new palace and help him marry the king's daughter. Eventually, when his father-in-law died, he became the new king.

This is obviously an imaginary story. But many people seem to view God as a magic genie. They expect Him to be available to grant their wishes whenever they need Him. When life is normal, they don't think much about Him. But when things go wrong, they can't understand why God doesn't drop everything else and come running to their aid.

This seems to have been Andrew's view of God. If that is our view as well, we should consider how God feels about this. It is selfish for us to expect God to bow to our every wish and bail us out every time we have a problem.

I suspect God would have told Andrew pretty much the same thing I did. "Find a financial advisor to help you set up a savings plan that will help you pay off your debts." Sometimes God helps us work our own way out of our problems. God could have snapped a finger and supplied Andrew with money to pay his debts. But God also knows that sometimes we need to learn some lessons that only difficult times will teach us.

I doubt that Andrew acquired any new gambling debts while working to pay off his old ones. I hope he also changed his view of God.

Is God a Fire Escape?

When is a fire escape not a fire escape?

Nothing is worse than a fire escape that fails you when you need it. A century or so ago a fire broke out in a tall multi-storied factory. Some of the people in the factory were on the wrong side of the building and couldn't reach the fire escape. These all died in the fire. But that wasn't the only problem. Several hundred people on the right side of the building crowded onto the fire escape, but unfortunately, it wasn't strong enough and tore away from the building.

I'm sure this was a terrifying experience. Just when they thought they had found a way of escape, it failed them. Many of the people on the fire escape fell screaming to their death.

What went wrong? Probably several things. First, someone had tried to save money by building the fire escape as cheaply as possible. And second, no one had bothered to maintain the fire escape. Since it had almost never been used, no one thought of maintaining it until it was too late.

A friend of mine worked in a factory some years ago. He noticed that some of his co-workers had their personal fire escapes. They carried a copy of the "sinner's prayer" in their pocket or their wallet. They wanted to be ready in case of a serious accident. They hoped they could quickly get ready to meet God by praying the sinner's prayer as they were dying. Apparently some of the rough and tough crowd he worked with were convinced that God and hell were real, and they didn't want to die unprepared. But they didn't want to live a Christian life, so they came up with an alternative plan.

The problem with a "fire-escape-god" is that when you really need Him, He might not be around. You might not be able to quickly find your paper or remember your prayer. While God is merciful, He has never promised to be a fire escape.

Fire escapes on factories or apartment buildings should be checked every week or so. Every few months they should be inspected in-depth, and every year they should be extensively tested. After all, lives may depend on it. Similarly, any person who wants God at his side in an emergency should regularly ensure that his relationship with Him is intact and in good condition.

Is God the "God of Jabez"?

A decade or two ago, someone read some obscure verses in 1 Chronicles 4 and wrote a book about them. We don't know much about the man called Jabez, but the Bible calls him honorable and records his prayer:

"Oh, that You would bless me indeed, and enlarge my territory, that Your hand would be with me, and that You would keep me from evil, that I may not cause pain!" (1 Chronicles 4:10).

God granted Jabez his request. The story takes up two verses, but sometimes people see a big opportunity in them. They use them as a formula that they think will trigger God's blessing on them, especially in material things. For instance, a well-known evangelical pastor wanted to build a new mega-church on a large piece of land beside an important interstate. So he drove out to where he could view the land and prayed a typical "name it and claim it" prayer over it, claiming God's blessing for the acquisition.

I'm not judging Jabez or his motives. Apparently God honored him. But many people in the last decade have tried to cash in on this discovery by using it to persuade God to give them things they want.

Perhaps the pastor above considered his motives good as well. I'm not judging him either. But instead of giving God orders or instructing Him about our wishes, wouldn't it be better to humbly come to God and ask for His direction? Maybe we should consider finding out how He feels about our idea. Perhaps He sees a danger in our plans that we haven't thought of. Maybe He knows it wouldn't be good for us. Or maybe He knows that we need to learn to submit to His plans for our own spiritual good.

I remember some years ago when a group of young men found Jesus. They wanted to tell others about their conversions and the blessing Jesus had been to them. So they decided to start a rock and roll singing group. They asked God to finance them with at least a million dollars so they could skyrocket the group to overnight fame. Then they planned to use this platform to witness for Jesus and win others to Him.

But it didn't work. God didn't cooperate. And later one of them admitted that it would have been one of the worst things that could have happened to them.

Sometimes God enlarges our spiritual coastline by limiting our material or financial boundaries.

Is God a "Health and Wealth" God?

Job was known as the greatest of all the people in the East. He was enormously wealthy. The Bible tells us that Abraham was also very rich in cattle, silver, and gold. But Solomon was even richer.

The Bible provides accounts of all three of these men,

but Solomon's story is perhaps the most interesting. He was crowned king of Israel when he was about twenty years old. One night soon after this, God came to him in a dream and asked him, "What shall I give you?"

Solomon replied, "Give me an understanding mind to govern your people, that I may discern between good and evil."

This pleased God, so He granted Solomon's request. He also gave him riches and honor. Solomon went on to become so rich that silver was almost worthless—as plenteous as stones.

As we read of these Old Testament characters, it is evident that God materially blessed those who followed Him. In fact, David wrote, "Delight yourself also in the Lord, And He shall give you the desires of your heart" (Psalm 37:4). Although we live in the New Testament era, some people still measure God's blessings in dollars and cents.

I had a relative who was very poor. So poor, in fact, that he went from bridge to bridge on small country roads trying to catch a few fish to keep food in the house. A relative once commented about him: "Doesn't he see that God isn't blessing him?" The implication being, of course, that people who have enough money and material things to be comfortable are being blessed by God because they are good Christians. By this thinking, those who aren't blessed like this are evidently *not* good Christians.

This philosophy is common. But is it Biblical? Jesus Christ said one day, "Foxes have holes and birds of the air have nests, but the Son of Man has nowhere to lay His head" (Matthew 8:20). He owned practically nothing. Nor did His apostles. They had to leave their businesses behind in order to follow Him.

Somehow this doesn't correlate very well with the concept of a "health and wealth" God.

Is God a Benevolent Grandfather?

C.S. Lewis said the following in his book, *The Problem of Pain*.

> What would really satisfy us would be a God who said of anything we happened to like doing, What does it matter so long as they are contented? We want, in fact, not so much a Father in heaven as a grandfather in heaven—a senile benevolence who, as they say, "liked to see young people enjoying themselves," and whose plan for the universe was simply that it might be truly said at the end of each day, "a good time was had by all."

Some people truly seem to feel this way about God. *Surely God won't worry about a few bad things I've done if I'm generally a good person.* They reason that if something makes sense to them, it probably does to God as well. Or, as one author wrote, "If you're a Christian, you don't need to feel guilty about sin—Jesus died for you."[1]

People justify many sinful things under the assumption that God is love and will surely overlook their sins. After all, God has pulled out His wallet and paid our debt Himself. Now He is happy and so am I. But the Bible paints a different picture. When people choose to live in deliberate sin, Christ's death has no power to save them unless they repent and stop practicing sin. In the judgment scenes given in the New Testament, God makes this clear, as in the following:

"Then I saw a great white throne and Him who sat on it, from whose face the earth and the heaven fled away. And there was found no place for them. And I saw the dead, small and great, standing before God, and books were opened. And another book was opened, which is the Book of Life. And the dead were judged according to their works, by the things which were written in the books. The sea gave up the dead who were in it, and Death and Hades delivered up the dead who were in them. And they were judged, each one according to his works" (Revelation 20:11-13).

....

There you have them—five imaginary gods that people

---

[1] This seems to be the main theme of the book *The Guilt Trip* by Hal Lindsey.

have concocted to make their lives easier. Do you serve one of them? Or perhaps another one you have pieced together that allows you to have what you want in life?

It seems most people don't want to serve a God who might tell them how to live and what to do. They much prefer a god who will serve *them*. This seems much more enjoyable.

For now, anyway . . .

Is God Angry? Vindictive?

For I, the LORD your God, am a jealous God, visiting the iniquity of the fathers upon the children to the third and fourth generations of those who hate Me, but showing mercy to thousands, to those who love Me and keep My commandments. Deuteronomy 5:9, 10

A few years ago, a former evangelical pastor-turned-atheist wrote a book lashing out at God. He called God a malevolent bully and many other nasty names.

Will this cause God to feel hurt and lash back?

Let's think about the nature of God that Job met in the whirlwind that day. I don't get the idea that He is too affected by what humanity thinks of Him. God knows that what we think won't change the facts. We ourselves are the ones who will suffer for such thoughts. God doesn't need to defend Himself. In Job's case, He only did so as a favor to Job.

God will not force anyone to serve Him. If someone wants to call Him a malevolent bully, he may do so.

However, we should note that God does have two sides to Him.

On the one hand, God is merciful, as the introductory passage from Deuteronomy states. Those who love Him and serve Him will live under His mercy.

But God has another side—His holiness and His hatred for sin—which these verses also portray. This is the side of God that today's society often fails to understand.

Many people, even Christians, think God is like the benevolent grandfather we talked about in the last chapter. But that is not an accurate picture of God at all. God is not worried about political correctness or trampling on people's toes. He is a God of character. He does what He does because it is the right thing to do.

Human leaders of democratic nations worry about voters' opinion of them. They worry about reelection and approval ratings. Sometimes they make changes to their platform to maintain their popularity. That is not how God is.

People don't understand real leadership anymore. That is one reason they don't understand God.

God constantly balances mercy and justice. All of us deserve punishment, but God would rather give us mercy. Because of this, He always offers mercy first. But when people reject mercy, they must live with the justice of God.

Does God get angry?

Yes.

Does He get angry when someone tortures an innocent child?

Yes.

Does He get angry when someone calls Him a malevolent bully?

Yes.

But His mercy and patience precede His anger and justice. People see this and fool themselves into thinking that either God doesn't exist, or He is a pushover that they can manipulate as they please.

Society today goes by feelings, not by facts. Punishing sin doesn't seem nice, so we try to deny God His right to punish sinners. But that isn't how things work. Someday there will be a culmination of all things, and God's anger will fall on those who have deliberately snubbed their noses at Him.

Hebrews 10:26-31 speaks of this. It summarizes it by saying, "It is a fearful thing to fall into the hands of the living God."

We have done serious harm to society and the church by trying to hide this side of God.

He is God Almighty, and we will never turn Him into anything else.

Manipulating God

Therefore understand that the LORD your God is not
giving you this good land to possess because of your
righteousness, for you are a stiff-necked people.
Deuteronomy 9:6

Some people have a habit of making others feel guilty in order to get their own way. They have become very good at it, and those around them know that the easiest way to get along with them is to let them have their own way.

It's really no surprise that people try to do the same thing with God.

Making God Feel Bad

A lot of people think they can coerce God into obeying them by trying to make Him feel bad. Consider these complaints . . .

> "God, you promised me a wife and a family. The Bible is clear this is your plan, but you've ignored me."

> "God, King David wrote that he had never seen the righteous forsaken, or his seed begging bread. Why aren't you supplying my needs?"

> "God, Psalm 37:4 says that if I delight myself in you, you will give me the desires of my heart. But you've been ignoring my prayers for . . ."

Can you see where we are going?

It's like the wife who tells her husband, "You never remember to give me flowers." And she pouts until he drives to town and gets her some.

Or it's like the boy who tells his mother, "You never let me go fishing with my friends. I'm tired of always working in the garden while everyone else enjoys their summer holidays." And he pouts until she finally lets him go. She does the work herself even though she is tired and sick. (In the story I'm thinking of, the mother died before he returned.)

Sometimes it seems to work, after a fashion, to try to put God on a guilt trip. In Psalm 106, the writer recounts the experience of the Israelites in the wilderness. The Israelites were tired of the manna God sent them and wanted meat—juicy, bloody meat they could chew on. They stood in the doorways of their tents, weeping like spoiled children. If ever someone tried to put God on a guilt trip, they did.

God let them have their way. Verse 15 says He gave them their request, but sent leanness into their soul. Similarly, God may give you what you want if you put Him on a guilt trip, but you will be responsible for the consequences.

Have any of us ever tried to put God on a guilt trip? I'm sure we have. But before we do it again, let's consider the possible consequences.

Reasoning with God

Just in case God hasn't noticed the good things you do for Him, perhaps you should tell Him. At least that seems to be how the Pharisee on the street corner reasoned. "God, I thank You that I am not like other men—extortioners, unjust, adulterers, or even as this tax collector. I fast twice a week; I give tithes of all that I possess" (Luke 18:9-14).

In case you don't remember the story, the tax collector stood down the street, ashamed to be seen. He knew how unworthy he was. He beat his breast and said, "God, be merciful to me, a sinner."

Jesus used this story to show His audience what God thought of people who tried to tell Him how good and how worthy they were. God accepted the tax collector, but it appears He didn't pay any attention to the Pharisee.

We can also get caught in this trap. We tell other people all about the good things we do. We even tell God about them. And then we wonder why God seems to ignore us. Jesus told us why this happens. He said that God exalts those who humble themselves and humbles those who exalt themselves.

God isn't impressed by the good things people do just to try to get His attention. God wants us to do good deeds, but the good deeds He notices are those that people do without thinking. They do them because they care or because they see a need. If we only do good things because we want a reward, our work is in vain (see Matthew 6:1-4).

Arguing with God

Job tried this. He challenged God to a debate in Job 23. We've already discussed the results of this.

Similarly, I know a man who watched as a hailstorm destroyed his crops. He stood in the middle of the road in front of his field and shook his fist at the sky. At God? Or just at the weather? I'm not sure, but how much difference is there? Did he think he was a good Christian and deserved better?

We can try arguing with God. But like Job, we will probably learn the hard way that God isn't intimidated by us feeble humans. God simply laid the evidence of His greatness in front of Job and Job crumbled.

The person who tries to manipulate God will always be the loser.

What Rights Does God Have?

Do not be deceived, God is not mocked; for whatever a man sows, that he will also reap. Galatians 6:7

Human rights is a big issue today. Social activists receive a lot of publicity. Women have rights; children have rights; minorities have rights; even animals have rights. Parents and teachers, however, don't have many rights, nor do churches. Nor do unborn babies. In fact, you can kill an unborn baby without repercussion, but if you would spank the child five years later, you might receive jail time. Criminals are protected from cruel and unusual punishments even after they have used cruel and unusual tortures to kill a victim.

Something seems backwards.

But, I wonder, what rights does God have?

Does God Have the Right to Say NO to Me?

While I was writing this book, I received a letter from a person I'll call Jack. Jack had drifted away from God, but then he decided to rebuild his relationship with Him and made a conscious effort to change his life.

I think Jack was serious. But he also had dreams of doing big things for God. He believed that by rebuilding his relationship with Him and changing his life, he would open the door for God to use him to do great things.

Instead, everything fell flat.

Jack was disappointed. Very disappointed. He was the victim of one of the most damaging myths passed around by Christians. It has some variations, but it goes something like this . . . *If you are careful to obey God's commands and do his will, He will reward you by giving you many blessings. He will answer your prayers and use you in mighty ways.*

I suggested to Jack that maybe God was more interested in his submission to God's will than in his great accomplishments.

I don't doubt that Jack had good intentions. But I think he had to admit that the idea of doing great things for God was very attractive. And one big reason it was attractive was because of the attention it would bring him.

That, very often, is the key. If we are really interested in bringing glory to God and serving Him, we need to get ourselves out of the way so that what we do will bring glory to God. God may ask us to do something quite humble, such as being the janitor in the local church instead of calling us to be the pastor. He might ask us to bring up godly children for Him instead of being part of an important counseling ministry.

This brings up another question:

Does God Have the Right to Rule My Life?

In the last decades, society has become extremely anti-authority. We don't like to be told what to do, even if it is for our own good. People fear to train their children to obey because it might be detrimental to their development. But it doesn't take long for a self-confident, egotistical teenager to turn into an anarchist.

This has rubbed off on Christianity. The young boy who tells his mother, "I have rights," as a twelve-year-old, will tell the police the same thing when he is sixteen or eighteen. And it won't be long until he tries to tell God as well.

This doesn't damage God, but it does damage the person who feels this way. And it damages the people he influences.

The person who thinks the government and society owe him a living is similar. Our welfare society has encouraged these feelings to the point where people consider them natural and valid. It will be a big shock to such people to face God and learn that they had responsibilities in life.

Does God Have the Right to Judge Me?

Many people struggle with this one. God tells me not to judge others but judges me. He tells me not to kill, but in the Old Testament He wiped out entire nations.

Several aspects enter this question. First, God is our Creator, and He wrote the rules. He does not need to fit into our expectations.

Second, God is our Judge. He has the right to judge men and women for their sin. The cases in the Old Testament that people usually point to are cases of nations being judged for sin, not illustrations of genocide. In all cases, the judgment followed centuries of mercy. If a judge in a country that allows capital punishment sentences a criminal to death, we don't accuse the judge of murder. He has merely done his duty.

We have access to God's "guidebook." We can read the Bible and understand His expectations. He has also put into our hearts the basic knowledge of good and evil, so even if we don't have a Bible, we understand that actions like murder and stealing are wrong. Judgment Day should not bring many surprises with it for us.

God Has the Right to Be God

One of the main things I want to emphasize in this book is that *God has the right to be God.* He clearly showed Job from a practical perspective that this is true. If you want a more abstract look at this subject, read Ecclesiastes as well. It has been said that Ecclesiastes is the philosophical backing for the Book of Job.

Both the Bible and human experience clarify that things work out better when we give God His rightful place in our lives. Everyone wins when this happens.

What Does God Expect of Me?

He has shown you, O man, what is good; and what does the LORD require of you but to do justly, to love mercy, and to walk humbly with your God? Micah 6:8

The focus of this book has been the question: What can I expect from God? In this chapter, I'd like to turn that around and ask a more important question: What does God expect of me?

This shift in focus turns everything upside down.

Is This Legalism?

We run into two extremes when we look at this part of this

subject. Some people assume that if they do enough good works, God will reward them by blessing them on earth and receiving them into heaven. We've already looked at some of that.

The other extreme is believing that once God saves us by His grace, our behavior doesn't matter because our salvation is secure.

As is often the case, the truth lies somewhere in between these two extremes. First, the Bible is clear that we are saved by grace. "Not by works of righteousness which we have done, but according to His mercy He saved us" (Titus 3:5). There is no such thing as a list of works or good deeds that will get us into heaven.

On the other hand, the Bible also tells us that "We are His workmanship, created in Christ Jesus for good works, which God prepared beforehand that we should walk in them" (Ephesians 2:10). We see that God does expect some things of us. He didn't save us just so we could continue to live in sin and do as we please.

Jesus said, "If you love me, keep my commandments." So what are these commandments? Let's take a quick look at a few of the things God expects of us. You can find these in 1 John, in the New Testament.

Walk in the Light

In the Bible, light often refers to truth and things that are good. Darkness often refers to sin and evil. God is completely light and has no darkness at all. Choosing light over darkness will also be the goal of all true followers of God.

According to 1 John 1: 5-10, walking in the light includes having fellowship with other Christians. It includes being cleansed from sin by the blood of Christ. It includes confessing our sins and being forgiven for them.

In other words, it means becoming someone totally different from what we were as sinners. It doesn't mean we will never fail, but it does mean we will confess our failures and bring them to Christ.

Abide in Christ

According to 1 John 2:1-6, Christ is our personal lawyer in the presence of God. When we fail, He is there to represent us. He earned the right to do this by dying for us. But in return for this, He asks several things of us.

We are to "abide in Him." John defines this as walking as Jesus did and keeping His commandments. Then he goes on and lists a few more commands for us.

Love One Another

John places love at the top of the list of requirements. Interestingly, he describes this as an old commandment dating back to the very beginning. Then he turns around and calls it a new commandment as well. In other words, loving our brother (other followers of God) has always been important and always will be. If we don't, we aren't walking in the light of Christ.

This is a big subject in 1 John, and he returns to it repeatedly. We ignore it to our own peril.

Do Not Love the World

John tells us next, "Do not love the world, or the things in the world."

In the Bible the world refers to the evil around us, and to the things that would draw us away from God. In 1 John 2:16, the Bible defines the things in the world as being the desires of our body (to do wrong things), the desires of our eyes (to look at things we shouldn't), and the pride of life (to think too highly of ourselves).

The world will soon be gone. We will die and leave it all behind. If that is what we have lived for, we will have nothing left. But if we love Christ and His ways instead of the world, we will have only begun to live when we die.

Test the Spirits

In chapter four, John warns us not to believe every spirit that would try to direct us. We are surrounded by false prophets, so it is important to make sure our advice comes from people who are genuine followers of Christ.

What Can I Expect from God?

For God is not unjust to forget your work and labor of love which you have shown toward His name, in that you have ministered to the saints, and do minister. Hebrews 6:10

By now you might be saying, "You have written this whole book and all you've done is tell me what I *can't* expect from God. Don't I get anything out of this?"

Absolutely. But first . . .

What Does God Owe Me?

This question starts out with an interesting assumption: "I

have some rights, some things I deserve, and God owes them to me."

We live in a world where people assume that they have a lot of rights. They have the right to a minimum standard of living. They have the right to be respected. They have the right to be considered innocent until proven guilty. They have the right to free health care. They have the right to be looked after by the government.

Human rights have become a huge political issue. In some cases, children have more rights than their parents, and criminals have more rights than their victims.

Maybe we shouldn't be surprised when people assume that they have some rights that even God can't override. For instance, I have the right to be married and have a family. I've been a good Christian and God should reward me for that.

Or, perhaps, I have the right to a comfortable standard of living.

Or I have the right to be healthy, and if I have enough faith, God will reward me with good health.

Like almost everything else, Christianity can become a selfish entity. We become Christians in order to escape hell, instead of becoming Christians because we realize that Jesus is worthy of our love and our service. We obey the Bible in order to get to heaven, when we should obey because Jesus is our Lord and our King, and we love and respect Him too much to disobey Him.

We so easily focus on ourselves rather than on Christ. But as we yield to God, that is something He will work on in our hearts. In the pictures of heaven John recorded in Revelation, we see a total focus on Christ and God. In Revelation 4, the elders cast their crowns before the throne saying, "You are worthy, O Lord, To receive glory and honor and power; For You created all things, And by Your will they exist and were created."

In Revelation 7, an enormous multitude stood before Christ and cried out, "Salvation belongs to our God who sits on the throne, and to the Lamb!" John asked the angel who these people were, and the angel replied that they were martyrs, those who had suffered great tribulation.

None of these people seemed to feel that God owed them anything. Instead, they expressed overflowing gratitude for what He had done for them. Many had died for Him. All of them had suffered "great tribulation."

I wonder how much sympathy these martyrs would have with us in our affluent society when we feel God doesn't give us everything we want.

We need to get our focus off ourselves and onto others. Especially we need to focus on our King—the One who died for us.

What Do You Get in Return?

1. **You will find rest.** The greatest invitation in the New Testament is found in Matthew 11:28-30. Jesus invites us to come to Him, take up His yoke, and find rest. How often have you wished for rest? Real rest?

   Genuine peace and rest can only be found in Christ.

2. **You will find fulfillment.** Very few people ever find fulfillment and meaning in life. That is because very few people truly allow Jesus to be their Lord and Master.

   Real fulfillment and meaning in life are found only by letting go and allowing Him to take control.

3. **You will find love.** Jesus told His disciples, "As the Father loved Me, I also have loved you; abide in My love. If you keep My commandments, you will abide in My love, just as I have kept My Father's commandments and abide in His love. These things I have spoken to you, that My joy may remain in you, and that your joy may be full" (John 15:9-11).

   True love is found only in Christ.

4. **You will be part of God's kingdom.** In His description of the judgment, Jesus said, "Then the King will say to those on His right hand, 'Come, you blessed of My Father, inherit the kingdom prepared for you

from the foundation of the world' " (Matthew 25:34).

You can only be part of God's kingdom by following the teachings of Christ.

5. **You will find grace.** Hebrews tells us, "Let us therefore come boldly to the throne of grace, that we may obtain mercy and find grace to help in time of need" (Hebrews 4:16). In the context of this verse, it is speaking of Christ sympathizing with our weaknesses and temptations. He understands what we face because He was once a man and faced such things as well.

Grace is our only hope of salvation and eternal peace.

In Conclusion . . .

God doesn't need me to defend Him. Nor does He need you. But God *wants* us. God had a reason for creating the world and putting Adam and Eve here. It seems He craved companionship. He desired a relationship with humans— with people who *wanted* to be His friends and *wanted* to serve Him. That is still His desire today.

Adam and Eve walked and talked with God in the cool of the evening. They had perfect friendship. But this utopia was shattered when Satan persuaded Eve to disobey God— all in search of an illusive pleasure called the knowledge of good and evil. Today, you and I have that knowledge. We also know the repercussions of it, especially the knowledge of evil. We can't get rid of this knowledge entirely, but with God's help, we can put it behind us. We can experience, somewhat at least, the relationship with God that Adam and Eve had.

That is worth more than anything else in this world.

Appendix: A Biblical Description of God

Behold, God is great, and we do not know Him; Nor can the number of His years be discovered. Job 36:26

Verses Describing God

Genesis 17:1 – I am Almighty God; walk before Me and be blameless.

Numbers 23:19 – God is not a man, that He should lie, nor a son of man, that He should repent. Has He said, and will He not do? Or has He spoken, and will He not make it good?

Deuteronomy 4:24 – For the LORD your God is a consuming fire, a jealous God.

Deuteronomy 4:31 – (For the LORD your God is a merciful God), He will not forsake you nor destroy you, nor forget the covenant of your fathers which He swore to them.

Deuteronomy 9:6 – Therefore understand that the LORD your God is not giving you this good land to possess because of your righteousness, for you are a stiff-necked people.

Deuteronomy 10:17 – For the LORD your God is God of gods and Lord of lords, the great God, mighty and awesome, who shows no partiality nor takes a bribe.

Deuteronomy 20:1 – When you go out to battle against your enemies, and see horses and chariots and people more numerous than you, do not be afraid of them; for the LORD your God is with you, who brought you up from the land of Egypt.

Deuteronomy 33:27 – The eternal God is your refuge, and underneath are the everlasting arms; He will thrust out the enemy from before you, and will say, 'Destroy!'

2 Chronicles 30:9 – For if you return to the LORD, your brethren and your children will be treated with compassion by those who lead them captive, so that they may come back to this land; for the LORD your God is gracious and merciful, and will not turn His face from you if you return to Him.

Job 9:4 – God is wise in heart and mighty in strength. Who has hardened himself against Him and prospered?

Job 36:5 – Behold, God is mighty, but despises no one; He is mighty in strength of understanding.

Job 36:22 – Behold, God is exalted by His power; who teaches like Him?

Job 36:26 – Behold, God is great, and we do not know Him; nor can the number of His years be discovered.

Ecclesiastes 5:2 – Do not be rash with your mouth, and let not your heart utter anything hastily before God. For God is in heaven, and you on earth; therefore let your words be few.

Ecclesiastes 8:17 – Then I saw all the work of God, that a man cannot find out the work that is done under the sun. For though a man labors to discover it, yet he will not find it; moreover, though a wise man attempts to know it, he will not be able to find it.

John 4:24 – God is Spirit, and those who worship Him must worship in spirit and truth.

1 Corinthians 1:9 – God is faithful, by whom you were called into the fellowship of His Son, Jesus Christ our Lord.

1 Corinthians 10:13 – No temptation has overtaken you except such as is common to man; but God is faithful, who will not allow you to be tempted beyond what you are able, but with the temptation will also make the way of escape, that you may be able to bear it.

1 Corinthians 14:33 – For God is not the author of confusion but of peace, as in all the churches of the saints.

Galatians 6:7 – Do not be deceived, God is not mocked; for whatever a man sows, that he will also reap.

Hebrews 6:10 – For God is not unjust to forget your work and labor of love which you have shown toward His name, in that you have ministered to the saints, and do minister.

1 John 1:5 – This is the message which we have heard from Him and declare to you, that God is light and in Him is no darkness at all.

1 John 3:20 – For if our heart condemns us, God is greater than our heart, and knows all things.

1 John 4:8 – He who does not love does not know God, for God is love.

About the Author

Lester Bauman was born into an Old Order Mennonite home close to Kitchener, Ontario. Later his family joined a local conservative Mennonite church. As a young-married man, he taught for five years in several Christian schools. Later he worked for thirteen years out of a home office for Rod and Staff Publishers, Inc. as a writer and editor. During this time, he and his wife Marlene moved with their family from Ontario to Alberta, where they live presently. They have six children and eleven grandchildren, and are members of a local Western Fellowship Mennonite Church.

During his time with Rod and Staff, Lester wrote ten books, including *The True Christian* and *God and Uncle Dale,* both available from Christian Aid Ministries. He spent a number of years in Alberta working as an HR manager in a corporate setting. He now works for the Christian Aid Ministries billboard evangelism ministry out of a home office, doing content writing for their website, answering correspondence, and writing resource materials.

Lester has written several other books published by Christian Aid Ministries: *Sylvester's Journal, What Is the Bible?, The Matthew Challenge,* and *Searching for Meaning.* He is working on additional books as time allows.

You can contact Lester through his personal website at www.lbauman.ca or by email at lester.bauman@gmail.com. You may also write to him in care of Christian Aid Ministries, P.O. Box 360, Berlin, Ohio 44610.

About Christian Aid Ministries

Christian Aid Ministries was founded in 1981 as a non-profit, tax-exempt 501(c)(3) organization. Its primary purpose is to provide a trustworthy and efficient channel for Amish, Mennonite, and other conservative Anabaptist groups and individuals to minister to physical and spiritual needs around the world. This is in response to the command to "Do good to all, especially to those who are of the household of faith" (Galatians 6:10).

Each year, CAM supporters provide 15–20 million pounds of food, clothing, medicines, seeds, Bibles, Bible story books, and other Christian literature for needy people. Most of the aid goes to orphans and Christian families. Supporters' funds also help to clean up and rebuild for natural disaster victims, put up Gospel billboards in the U.S., support several church-planting efforts, operate two medical clinics, and provide resources for needy families to make their own living. CAM's main purposes for providing aid are to help and encourage God's people and bring the Gospel to a lost and dying world.

CAM has staff, warehouses, and distribution networks in Romania, Moldova, Ukraine, Haiti, Nicaragua, Liberia, Israel, and Kenya. Aside from management, supervisory personnel, and bookkeeping operations, volunteers do most of the work at CAM locations. Each year, volunteers at our warehouses, field bases, Disaster Response Services projects, and other locations donate over 200,000 hours of work.

CAM's ultimate purpose is to glorify God and help enlarge His kingdom. "Whatever you do, do all to the glory of God" (1 Corinthians 10:31).